Guitar Chord Songbook

Green Day

Cover photo © MARKA/Alamy

ISBN 978-1-4768-1697-5

Visit Hal Leonard Online at
www.halleonard.com

Contact us:
Hal Leonard
7777 West Bluemound Road
Milwaukee, WI 53213
Email: info@halleonard.com

In Europe, contact:
Hal Leonard Europe Limited
42 Wigmore Street
Marylebone, London, W1U 2RN
Email: info@halleonardeurope.com

In Australia, contact:
Hal Leonard Australia Pty. Ltd.
4 Lentara Court
Cheltenham, Victoria, 3192 Australia
Email: info@halleonard.com.au

Guitar Chord Songbook

Contents

American Idiot

Words by Billie Joe
Music by Green Day

Melody:

Don't want to be an A-mer - i-can id-i-ot.

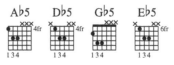

A♭5   D♭5   G♭5   E♭5

Intro

‖: A♭5 D♭5 G♭5 | D♭5 A♭5 G♭5 |
| A♭5 D♭5 G♭5 | D♭5 A♭5 N.C. :‖

Verse 1

N.C.   A♭5 D♭5 G♭5 D♭5 A♭5 G♭5
Don't want to be an American idiot.

N.C.   A♭5 D♭5 G♭5 D♭5 A♭5 N.C.
Don't want a nation under the new media.

N.C.   A♭5 D♭5 G♭5 D♭5 A♭5 G♭5
Hey, can you hear the sound of hysteria?

N.C.   A♭5 D♭5 G♭5 D♭5 A♭5 N.C.
The subliminal mind-fuck, America.

Chorus 1

D♭5
Welcome to a new kind of tension

A♭5
All across the alienation

E♭5   A♭5
Where ev'rything isn't meant to be okay.

D♭5
Television dreams of tomorrow,

A♭5
We're not the ones who're meant to follow,

E♭5   N.C.
For that's enough to argue.

Interlude 1	Ab5 Db5 Gb5 | Db5 Ab5 Gb5 |
	Ab5 Db5 Gb5 | Db5 Ab5 N.C. |

Verse 2

N.C.   Ab5 Db5 Gb5 Db5 Ab5 Gb5
Well, maybe I'm the faggot America.

N.C.   Ab5 Db5 Gb5 Db5 Ab5 N.C.
I'm not a part of a redneck agenda.

N.C.   Ab5 Db5 Gb5 Db5 Ab5 Gb5
Now, ev'rybody, do the propaganda,

N.C.   Ab5 Db5 Gb5 Db5 Ab5 N.C.
And sing along to the age of paranoia.

Chorus 2   *Repeat Chorus 1*

Interlude 2   *Repeat Intro*

Guitar Solo

Db5 |	Ab5 |	|
Eb5 |	Ab5 |	|
Db5 |	Ab5 |	Eb5 | |
Ab5 Db5 Gb5 | Db5 Ab5 Gb5 |		
Ab5 Db5 Gb5 | Db5 Ab5 N.C. |		

Verse 3

A♭5   D♭5   G♭5 D♭5   G♭5
Don't want to be an A - meri - can idiot,

A♭5   D♭5   G♭5 D♭5 A♭5 G♭5
One na - tion controlled by the   me - di - a.

A♭5   D♭5   G♭5   D♭5 G♭5
Infor - mation age of hyster - ia

N.C.
Is calling out to idiot America.

Chorus 3

D♭5
Welcome to a new kind of tension

A♭5
All across the alienation

E♭5   A♭5
Where ev'rything isn't meant to be okay.

D♭5
Television dreams of tomorrow,

A♭5
We're not the ones who're meant to follow,

E♭5
For that's enough to argue.

Outro

‖: A♭5   D♭5   G♭5 | D♭5 A♭5 N.C. |
| A♭5   D♭5   G♭5 | D♭5 A♭5 G♭5 :‖
| A♭5   D♭5   G♭5 | D♭5 A♭5 N.C. |

Boulevard of Broken Dreams

Words by Billie Joe
Music by Green Day

Melody:

I walk a lone-ly road,

Fm   Ab   Eb   Bb   Ab/C   Db   C   Bb/D   E

Intro   ‖: Fm Ab | Eb Bb :‖

Verse 1

Fm   Ab
I walk a lonely road,

    Eb   Bb   Fm
The only one that I have ever known.

        Ab   Eb   Bb
Don't know where it goes, but it's home to me

        Fm   Ab Eb Bb
And I walk alone.

Fm   Ab
I walk this empty street

Eb   Bb   Fm
On the boule - vard of broken dreams,

        Ab   Eb   Bb
Where the city sleeps and I'm the only one

        Fm   Ab
And I walk alone.

Eb   Bb   Fm   Ab
I walk alone, I walk alone.

Eb   Bb   Ab/C
I walk alone, I walk a…

Chorus 1

D♭ A♭   E♭   Fm
My shadow's the only one that ___ walks beside me.

D♭ A♭ E♭   Fm
My shallow heart's the only ___ thing that's beating.

D♭   A♭ E♭   Fm
Some - times I wish someone out ___ there will find me.

D♭   A♭   C
'Till then I walk alone.

Fm   A♭   E♭   B♭
Ah. ___ Ah. ___ Ah. ___ Ah. Ah.

Fm   A♭   E♭   B♭
Ah. ___ Ah. ___ Ah.

Verse 2

Fm   A♭
I'm walking down the line

E♭   B♭   Fm
That divides me somewhere in my mind.

        A♭   E♭
On the borderline of the edge

    B♭   Fm   A♭ E♭ B♭
And where I walk alone.

Fm   A♭
Read be - tween the lines

E♭   B♭   Fm
Of what's fucked up and everything's al - right.

              A♭
Check my vital signs

      E♭   B♭   Fm   A♭
And know I'm still a - live and I walk alone.

E♭   B♭   Fm   A♭
I walk a - lone, I walk alone.

E♭   B♭   A♭/C
I walk a - lone, I walk a...

Chorus 2

Db Ab   Eb   Fm
My shadow's the only one that ___ walks beside me.

Db Ab   Eb   Fm
My shallow heart's the only ___ thing that's beating.

Db   Ab Eb   Fm
Some - times I wish someone out ___ there will find me.

Db   Ab   C
'Till then I walk alone.

Fm   Ab   Eb   Bb
Ah. ___ Ah. ___ Ah. ___ Ah. Ah.

Fm   Ab   Eb   Bb   Ab/C
Ah. ___ Ah. ___ I walk a - lone. I walk a…

Guitar Solo

‖: Db Ab |Eb   Fm :‖ *Play 3 times*
| Db Ab |C | |

Verse 3

Fm   Ab
I walk this empty street

Eb   Bb   Fm
On the boule - vard of broken ___ dreams,

          Ab
Where the city sleeps

     Eb   Bb   Ab/C
And I'm the only one and I walk a…

Chorus 3

Db Ab   Eb   Fm
My shadow's the only one that ___ walks beside me.

Db Ab   Eb   Fm
My shallow heart's the only thing that's beating.

Db   Ab Eb   Fm
Some - times I wish someone out ___ there will find me.

Db   Ab   C
'Till then I walk alone.

Outro

‖: Fm Db |Eb Bb/D |Ab   E   :‖ *Play 3 times*
| Fm Db |Eb Bb/D |Ab E N.C. |

Basket Case

Words by Billie Joe
Music by Green Day

Melody:

Do you have the time

Tune down 1/2 step:
(low to high) E♭-A♭-D♭-G♭-B♭-E♭

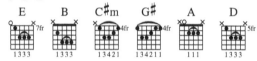

E   B   C#m   G#   A   D

Verse 1

E   B   C#m   G#
Do you have the time to listen to me whine

    A   E   B
A - bout nothing and ev'rything all at once?

E   B   C#m   G#
I am one of those me - lodramatic fools;

    A   E   B
Neu - rotic to the bone, no doubt about it.

Chorus 1

A   B   E
Sometimes I give myself the creeps.

A   B   E
Sometimes my mind plays tricks on me.

    A   B
It all keeps adding up.

    E   D   C#m
I think I'm cracking up.

    A   B   E
Am I just para - noid? Am I just stoned?

Interlude 1

‖: E   B   C#m | B   :‖

Verse 2

    E   B   C#m   G#
I went to a shrink to analyze my dreams.

      A   E   B
She says it's a lack of sex that's bringing me down.

    E   B   C#m   G#
I went to a whore, he said my life's a bore.

      A   E   B
So quit whining 'cause it's bringing her down.

Chorus 2

 A   B   E
  Sometimes I give myself the creeps.

 A   B   E
  Sometimes my mind plays tricks on me.

  A   B
It all keeps adding up.

  E   D   C#m
I think I'm cracking up.

   A   B   E
Am I just para - noid? Yeah, yeah, yeah.

Interlude 2   *Repeat Interlude 1*

Bridge

A   B   E
Grasping to con - trol so I better hold on.

Instrumental

‖: E   B | | C#m G# | |
| A   E | | B | :‖

Chorus 3   *Repeat Chorus 1*

Outro

‖: E | C#m | A   E B | :‖ *Play 4 times*
| A   E B | |

Brain Stew

(The Godzilla Remix)
from the TriStar Motion Picture
GODZILLA

Words by Billie Joe
Music by Green Day

Melody:

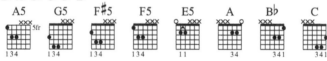

I'm hav-ing trou - ble try'n' to sleep.

Tune down 1/2 step:
(low to high) Eb-Ab-Db-Gb-Bb-Eb

A5	G5	F#5	F5	E5	A	Bb	C

Intro ‖: A5 N.C. G5 N.C. │ F#5 N.C. F5 N.C. E5 N.C. :‖

Verse 1

A5 N.C.   G5 N.C.   F#5 N.C. F5 N.C. E5 N.C.
I'm having trou - ble try'n' to sleep.

A5 N.C.   G5 N.C.   F#5 N.C. F5 N.C. E5 N.C.
I'm countin' sheep ___ but runnin' out.

A5 N.C.   G5 N.C. F#5 N.C.   F5 N.C. E5 N.C.
As time ticks by,   still I try.

A5 N.C.   G5 N.C.   F#5 N.C.
No rest for cross - tops in my mind.

F5   N.C. E5   N.C.
On my own, here we go.

Interlude 1 ‖: A5 N.C. G5 N.C. │ F#5 N.C. F5 N.C. E5 N.C. :‖

Verse 2

A5 N.C.   G5 N.C.   F$\sharp$5 N.C. F5 N.C. E5 N.C.
My eyes feel like ___ they're gonna bleed.

A5 N.C.   G5 N.C.   F$\sharp$5 N.C. F5 N.C. E5 N.C.
Dried up and bulg - ing out my skull.

A5 N.C.   G5 N.C. F$\sharp$5 N.C.   F5   N.C. E5 N.C.
My mouth is dry, ___   my face is numb.

A5 N.C.   G5 N.C.   F$\sharp$5 N.C.
Fucked up and spun ___ out in my room.

F5   E5
On my own, here we go.

Interlude 2   *Repeat Interlude 1*

Verse 3

A5 N.C.   G5 N.C.   F$\sharp$5 N.C. F5 N.C. E5 N.C.
My mind is set ___ on overdrive.

A5 N.C.   G5 N.C.   F$\sharp$5 N.C. F5 N.C. E5 N.C.
The clock is laugh - ing in my face.

A5 N.C.   G5 N.C. F$\sharp$5 N.C.   F5   N.C. E5 N.C.
A crooked spine, ___   my senses dulled.

A5 N.C.   G5 N.C.   F$\sharp$5 N.C. F5   E5
Past the point of ___ deliri - um.   On my own, here we go.

Interlude 3   ‖: A5 N.C. G5 N.C. | F$\sharp$5 N.C. F5 N.C. E5 N.C. :‖
                   ‖: A | B$\flat$ C   :‖

Verse 4   *Repeat Verse 2*

Outro   ‖:A5   G5 |F$\sharp$5   F5   E5   :‖ *Play 6 times*
             ‖:A5 | | | :‖ *Repeat and fade*

East Jesus Nowhere

Words by Billie Joe
Music by Green Day

Melody:

Raise your hands now to tes - ti - fy. __

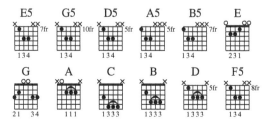

E5 G5 D5 A5 B5 E

G A C B D F5

Intro ‖: E5 G5 E5 D5 | E5 :‖ *Play 7 times*
| E5 G5 E5 D5 | E5 D5 A5 |

Verse
E5   D5 A5
   Raise your hands now to testify.

E5   D5 A5
   Your confession will be crucified.

E5   D5 A5
   You're a sacrificial suicide,

E5   D5
   Like a dog that's been sodo - mized.

A5   E5 G5   E5 D5 E5
   Well,   stand ___ up!   All the white boys.

G5 E5 D5   E5
Sit ___ down!   And the black girls.

G5   E5 D5 E5
Stand ___ up!   You're the soldiers.

G5 E5 D5   E5   D5 A5
Sit ___ down!   Of the new world.

Pre-Chorus 1

B5   D5 A5
Put your faith in a miracle

B5   D5 A5
And it's nondenominational.

B5   D5 A5
Join the choir, we'll be singing

B5   D5
In the church of wishful thinking.

Chorus 1

E   G
A fire burns to - day

A   C   B
Of blasphemy and geno - cide.

E   G
The sirens of de - cay

A   C   D
Will infiltrate the faith fa - natics.

Interlude 1

‖: E5 G5 E5 D5 |E5   :‖ *Play 3 times*

|E5 G5 E5 D5 |E5   D5   A5 |

Bridge

E   G   B
Oh, bless me, Lord, for I have sinned.

E   G   B
It's been a lifetime since I last confessed.

E   G   B
I threw my crutches in the river of a shadow of doubt.

E   G   B   D5 A5
And I'll be dressed up in my Sunday best.

Pre-Chorus 2

B5   D5 A5
Say a prayer for the family.

B5   D5 A5
Drop a coin for humanity.

B5   D5 A5
Ain't this uniform so flattering?

B5   D5
I never asked you a goddamn thing.

Chorus 2

Repeat Chorus 1

| Interlude 2 | ‖:E5 G5 E5 D5 |E5   :‖ *Play 4 times* |

E5
   Don't test me.

   Second guess me.

   Protest me.
                        D5 A5
   You will disap - pear.

Pre-Chorus 3

B5   D5 A5
   I want to know who's allowed to breed;

B5   D5 A5
   All the dogs who never learned to read,

B5   D5 A5
   Missionary politicians,

B5   D5
   And the cops of the new religion.

| **Guitar Solo** | \|E   \|G   \|A   \|C B \| |
| | \|E   \|G   \|A   \|C D \| |

| **Interlude 3** | ‖:E5   \| \|F5 \|E5 :‖ *Play 4 times* |

Chorus 3

   E5   G
A fire burns to - day

     A   C   B
Of blasphemy and geno - cide.

     E   G
The sirens of de - cay

     A   C B
Will infiltrate the in - side.

Outro	‖:E5 G5 E5 D5 |E5 :‖ *Play 3 times*
	|E5 G5 E5 D5 |E5 D5 A5 |
	|E5 | N.C. |

Holiday

Words by Billie Joe
Music by Green Day

Hear the sound of the fall - ing rain

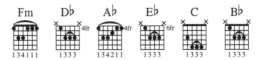

Intro

| Fm Db | Ab Eb | Fm Db | Ab Eb |
| Fm Db | Ab Eb | Fm Db | Ab Eb |

Say,   hey,   cha.

| Fm Db | Ab Eb | Fm Db | Ab Eb |

Verse 1

Fm   Db   Ab   Eb
Hear the sound of the falling rain

Fm   Db   Ab   C   Fm
Coming down like an Arma - geddon flame. (Hey.)

Db   Ab   Eb   C
The shame, the ones who died with - out a name.

Fm   Db   Ab   Eb
Hear the dogs howling out of key

Fm   Db   Ab   C   Fm
To a hymn called "Faith and mis - ery," (Hey.)

Db   Ab   Eb   C
And bleed, the company lost the war today.

	Fm Db Ab Eb

Chorus 1

        Fm   Db   Ab   Eb
I beg to dream and differ from the hollow lies.

        Fm   Db   Ab   C
This is the dawning of the rest of our lives on holiday.

Interlude 1   ‖:Fm Db |Ab Eb :‖

Verse 2

        Fm   Db   Ab   Eb
Hear the drum pounding out of time,

        Fm   Db   Ab   C   Fm
Another protest - er has crossed the line (Hey.)

        Db   Ab   Eb   C
To find the money's on the other side.

        Fm   Db   Ab   Eb   Fm
Can I get an - other "A - men?" (A - men.)

               Db   Ab   C   Fm
There's a flag wrapped around a score of men. (Hey.)

        Db   Ab   Eb   C
A gag, a plastic bag on a monument.

Chorus 2   *Repeat Chorus 1*

Interlude 2   ‖:Fm Ab |Db Bb Eb C |Fm Ab |Eb C Fm   :‖
                                                   Hey!

Guitar Solo |Db |Ab |C |Fm Eb |
                    |Db |Ab |C | |
                    | | |

Interlude 3 |Fm Ab |Db Bb Eb C |Fm Ab |Eb C Fm |
                    |Fm Ab |Db Bb Eb C |Fm Ab |Eb C Fm |
                                  The Representative from California has the floor.

Bridge   ‖:Fm A♭ |D♭ B♭ E♭ C |Fm A♭ |E♭ C Fm :‖ *Play 4 times*

Zieg Heil to the President gasman, bombs away is your punishment.

Pulverize the Eiffel Towers, who criticize your government.

Bang, bang goes the broken glass and kill all the fags that don't agree.

Trials by fire setting fire is not a way that's meant for me. Meant for me?
C
   Just 'cause… Just 'cause, because we're outlaws, yeah.

         Fm   D♭   A♭   E♭
Chorus 3   I beg to dream and differ from the hollow lies.
         Fm   D♭   A♭   C
   This is the dawning of the rest of our lives.
         Fm   D♭   A♭   E♭
   I beg to dream and differ from the hollow lies.
         Fm   D♭   A♭   C
   This is the dawning of the rest of our lives.…

   This is our lives on holiday.

Outro   ‖:Fm D♭ |A♭   E♭ :‖ *Play 3 times*
        |Fm D♭ |E♭ C Fm |

Geek Stink Breath

Words by Billie Joe
Music by Green Day

Melody:

I'm on a mis - sion, I made

Tune down 1/2 step:
(low to high) Eb-Ab-Db-Gb-Bb-Eb

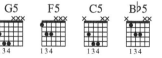

G5   F5   C5   Bb5

Intro

‖: G5 F5 C5 | G5 F5 C5 :‖
‖: G5 F5 | G5 F5   :‖

Verse 1

    G5 F5   G5   F5
I'm on a mission, I made my de - cision,

        G5   F5   G5 F5
Lead a path of self destruct - tion.

    G5   F5   G5   F5
A slow pro - gression, killing my com - plexion

        G5   F5   G5
And it's rotting out my teeth.

Pre-Chorus 1

Bb5   F5 Bb5   F5
  I'm on a roll, no self-con - trol,

    Bb5   F5   Bb5   F5
I'm ___ blowing off ___ steam with meth - ampheta - mine.

Chorus 1

        G5   F5
Well, don't know what I want

        G5   F5
And that's all that I've got,

        G5   F5   G5   F5 G5 F5
And I'm picking scabs off my face.

Verse 2

```
G5    F5    G5           F5
Ev'ry hour my blood is turning sour

       G5           F5   G5   F5
And my pulse is beating out of time.

   G5    F5    G5           F5
I found a treasure filled with sick pleasure

       G5    F5    G5
And it sits on a thin white line.
```

Pre-Chorus 2   *Repeat Pre-Chorus 1*

Chorus 2

```
         G5         F5
Well, don't know what I want

       G5         F5
And that's all that I've got,

       G5         F5   G5
And I'm picking scabs off my face.
```

Interlude   ‖: G5 F5   C5 | G5 F5   C5   :‖ *Play 4 times*

Verse 3

```
   G5  F5    G5           F5
I'm on a mission, I got no de - cision,

       G5           F5   G5  F5
Like a cripple running the rat race.

G5    F5           G5           F5
Wish in one hand and shit in the other,

       G5         F5    G5
And see which one gets filled first.
```

Pre-Chorus 3   *Repeat Pre-Chorus 1*

Chorus 3   *Repeat Chorus 2*

Outro

```
‖: G5   F5   C5   | G5   F5   C5   :‖
 | G5   F5   C5   | G5   F5   C5   | G5           |
   Geek           stink            breath.
```

Give Me Novacaine

Words by Billie Joe
Music by Green Day

Melody:

Take a-way the sen - sa - tion _ in - side, _____

A   F#m   Bm   E   D   F#5   B5   G#5   A5

Intro |A |F#m |Bm |E |

Verse 1
      A   F#m
Take away the sensation in - side,

  Bm   E
Bittersweet migraine in my head.

     A   F#m
It's like a throbbing toothache of the mind.

  Bm   E
I can't take this feeling anymore.

Chorus 1
  D   A
   Drain the pressure from the swell - ing.

  D   A
   The sensation's overwhelm - ing.

  D   F#5
Give me a long kiss goodnight and ev'rything will be alright,

  B5   E
Tell me that I won't feel a thing,

                A F#m Bm E
So give me novacaine.

Verse 2

```
A                     F#m
Out of body and out of mind,

Bm                          E
Kiss the demons out of my dreams.

 A                              F#m
I get the funny feeling that it's al - right,

Bm                          E
Jimmy says it's better than here.


I'll tell you why.
```

Chorus 2

```
D                             A
   Drain the pressure from the swell - ing.

D                        A
   The sensation's overwhelm - ing.

D                        F#5
Give me a long kiss goodnight and ev'rything will be alright,

B5                          E                       A
Tell me that I won't feel a thing, ___ so give me novacaine.
              G#5
Ah, nova - caine.
```

Guitar Solo

```
|F#5     |A5   G#5|F#5     |A5   G#5|
|F#5     |A5      |B5      |E       |
```

Chorus 3

```
D                             A
   Drain the pressure from the swell - ing.

D                        A
   The sensation's overwhelm - ing.

D                        F#5
Give me a long kiss goodnight and ev'rything will be alright,

B5                          E
Tell me, Jimmy, I won't feel a thing, ___ so give me novacaine.
```

Outro

```
|A       |F#m     |Bm      |
|E       |A       |        |
```

Good Riddance
(Time of Your Life)

Words by Billie Joe
Music by Green Day

Melody:
An - oth - er turn - ing point, _

G5   Csus2   D5   Em   D   G

Intro   ‖: G5 | | Csus2 | D5   :‖

Verse 1
    G5   Csus2   D5
    Another turning point, a fork ____ stuck in the road.

    G5   Csus2   D5
    Time grabs you by the wrist, directs ____ you where to go.

    Em   D5   Csus2   G5
    So make the best ____ of this test ____ and don't ask why.

    Em   D5   Csus2   G5
    It's not a ques - tion, but a les - son learned in time.

Chorus 1
          Em   G5
    It's something unpredict - able

          Em   G5
    But in the end is right.

          Em   D   G5 Csus2 D5 G5 Csus2 D5
    I hope you had the time ____ of your life.

	G5	**Csus2**	**D5**
Verse 2	So take the photographs and still frames ___ in your mind.		

G5   **Csus2**   **D5**
Hang it on a shelf in good ___ health and good time.

Em   **D5**   **Csus2**   **G5**
Tattoos of mem - ories, and dead ___ skin on trial.

Em   **D5**   **Csus2**   **G5**
For what it's worth, ___ it was worth ___ all the while.

Chorus 2   *Repeat Chorus 1*

Instrumental   *Repeat Verse 1 (Instrumental)*

Chorus 3   *Repeat Chorus 1*

                     Em   **G5**
Chorus 4   It's something unpredict - able

                     Em   **G5**
But in the end is right.

                      Em
I hope you had

                   D   **G5 Csus2 D5 G5 Csus2 D5 G5**
The time ___ of your life.

Hitchin' a Ride

Words by Billie Joe
Music by Billie Joe and Green Day

Melody:

Hey, Mis - ter, where you head - ed?

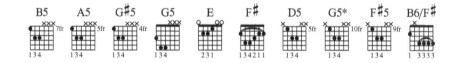

B5   A5   G#5   G5   E   F#   D5   G5*   F#5   B6/F#

Intro
‖: B5   A5 |G#5   G5 :‖

Verse 1

B5   A5   G#5   G5
Hey, Mister, where you headed?

B5   A5 G#5   G5
Are you in a hurry?

B5   A5 G#5   G5
I need a lift to happy hour,

B5 A5 G#5 G5
Say, oh no.

B5   A5   G#5   G5
Do you break for distilled spirits?

B5   A5   G#5 G5
I need a break as well.

B5   A5   G#5 G5
The well that inebri - ates the guilt.

B5   A5 G#5   G5
One, two. One, two, three, four.

Interlude 1
‖: B5   A5 |G#5   G5 :‖ *Play 3 times*
| B5   A5 |G#5   N.C. |

Verse 2

B5   A5   G#5   G5
Cold turkey's getting stale,

B5   A5   G#5   G5
Tonight I'm eating crow.

B5   A5   G#5   G5
Fer - mented salmon - ella,

    B5   A5   G#5   G5
Poison oak, no.

B5   A5   G#5   G5
There's a drought at the fountain of youth,

B5   A5   G#5   G5
And now I'm dehy - drated.

B5   A5   G#5   G5
My tongue is swelling up, I say,

B5   A5   G#5   G5
One, two. One, two, three, four.

Interlude 2

‖: B5   A5 |G#5   G5   :‖   *Play 4 times*

Chorus 1

E   F#   B5   A5   G#5 G5
Troubled times, you know I cannot lie.

E   F#
I'm off the wagon and I'm hitchin' a ride.

Interlude 3

‖: B5   A5 |G#5   G5   :‖

Verse 3

B5   A5   G#5   G5
There's a drought at the fountain of youth,

B5   A5   G#5   G5
And now I'm dehy - drated.

B5   A5   G#5   G5   N.C.
My tongue is swelling up, I say...

Guitar Solo

‖: B5   D5 |G5*   F#5   :‖   *Play 8 times*

Chorus 2

Repeat Chorus 1

Outro

‖: B5   D5 |G5*   F#5   :‖   *Play 7 times*
   Ride.   Hichin' a

| B5   A5 |G#5   N.C. |B6/F# |
   Ride.

In the End

Words by Billie Joe
Music by Green Day

Melody:

All brawn and _ no brains

Tune down 1/2 step:
(low to high) E♭-A♭-D♭-G♭-B♭-E♭

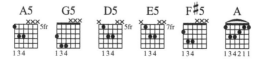

A5   G5   D5   E5   F♯5   A

Verse 1

      A5   G5   A5   G5
All brawn and no brains and all those nice things, yeah,

    A5 G5   A5
You finally got what you want.

G5 A5   G5   A5   G5
   Someone to look good with and light your cigarette.

A5   G5   A5
Is this what you really want?

Chorus 1

D5   E5
  I figured out   what you're all about

     A5   F♯5
And I don't think I like what I see.

    N.C. D5   E5
So,   I hope I won't be there in the end

            A5   G5 A5 G5
If you come a - round.

Verse 2

```
        A5           G5          A5
How long will he last before he's a creep

G5        A5           G5          A5
In the past and you're a - lone once a - gain?

G5   A5      G5       A5        G5
   Will you pop up again and be my spe - cial friend

    A5           G5          A5
'Till the end, and when will that be?
```

Chorus 2

```
D5              E5
   I figured out    what you're all about

    A5                      F#5
And I don't think I like what I see.

    N.C.  D5                E5
So,     I hope I won't be there in the end

            A5    G5 A5 G5 A5 G5 A5 G5
If you come a - round.
```

Interlude

```
‖: N.C.(A)  |(G5)      |(A)       |(G5)      :‖  Play 7 times
|(A)        |(G5)      |A5        |          |
```

Chorus 3

```
D5              E5
   I figured out    what you're all about

    A5                      F#5
And I don't think I like what I see.

    N.C.  D5                E5
So,     I hope I won't be there in the end

            A5    G5 A5 G5 A5 G5 A5
If you come a - round.
```

J.A.R.
(Jason Andrew Relva)
Words by Mike Dirnt
Music by Green Day

Melody:

My friend drove off ___ the oth - er

Tune down 1/2 step:
(low to high) Eb-Ab-Db-Gb-Bb-Eb

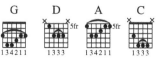

G   D   A   C

Intro

| N.C.(G) (D) | (A)   (D) | (G)   (D) | (A)   D   A |
|:G   A | | G   D | A   :|

Verse 1

G   A   G
  My friend drove off the other day,

         D   A   G
And now he's gone and all they say

       A   G D A
Is you gotta live 'cause life goes on.

G   A   G
  But now I see I'm mortal too,

       D   A   G
I can't live my life like you,

       A   G D A
Gotta live it up while life goes on.

Chorus 1

```
  G              D
And I think it's al - right
              A
That I do what I like,
                        G  D
'Cause that's the way I wanna live.
              A
And so I give, and I'm still...
```

Interlude 1

```
|G    D   |A    D   |G    D   |A    D    A |
 Giving.
```

Verse 2

```
G       A         G
  But now I wonder 'bout my friend,
      D     A    G
If you gave all he could give,
                  A       G    D A
'Cause he lived his life like I live mine.
G       A         G
  If you could see inside my head,
      D     A    G
Then you'd start to under - stand
              A       G    D A
The things I value in my heart.
```

Chorus 2   *Repeat Chorus 1*

Interlude 2

```
|G    D   |A    D   |G    D   |A    D   |
 Giving.
|G    D   |A    D   |G    D   |A    D   |
```

GREEN DAY   **31**

Bridge	C G D A You know that, I know that
	C G A D A You're watching me.
Guitar Solo	‖: G A | | G D | A :‖ *Play 4 times*
Chorus 3	*Repeat Chorus 1*
Interlude 3	*Repeat Interlude 2*
Outro	N.C.(G) (D) Gotta make a plan,
	(A) (D) Gotta do what's right,
	(G) (D) Can't run around in circles
	(A) (D) If you wanna build a life.
	(G) (D) But I don't wanna make a plan
	(A) (D) For a day far away,
	(G) (D) While I'm young and while I'm able
	(A) (D) All I wanna do is…

Know Your Enemy

Words by Billie Joe
Music by Green Day

Melody:

Do you know the en - e - my?

Chords: B E A F# F#5 B5

Intro   ‖: B E B | E B A :‖

Chorus 1

        B   E   B
Do you know the en - emy?

              E   B
Do you know your en - emy?

A   B   E   B   F#
Well, gotta know the en - emy. (Rah, eh!)

Verse 1

        B   E   B   E   B
Vi'lence is an en - ergy, against the en - emy,

A   B   E   B   F#
Well vi'lence is an en - ergy, (Rah eh!)

        B   E   B   E   B
Bringing on the fu - ry, the choir ____ in - fantry,

A   B   E   B   F#
Re - volt against the hon - or to o - bey. (Oh eh, oh eh.)

Verse 2

```
B        E   B         E     B
Overthrow the eff - igy, the vast major - ity,

A   B         E        B        F#
Well, burning down the fore - man of con - trol. (Oh eh, oh eh.)

B      E    B         E       B
Silence is the en - emy, against your ur - gency,

A B      E       B           F#
So rally up the de - mons of your soul. (Oh eh, oh eh.)
```

Chorus 2

```
    B         E     B
||: Do you know the en - emy?

              E     B
Do you know your en - emy?

A    B       E     B         F#
Well, gotta know the en - emy. (Rah, eh!) :||
```

Bridge 1

```
      E           B
The in - surgency will rise

          E                 B
When the blood's been sacri - ficed.

          E              B
We'll be blinded by the lies

      F#5  B5  F#5  B5  F#5
In your eyes.              Say!
```

Guitar Solo

```
||: B    E B  |    E  A | B    E B | F#           :||
                                     (Oh eh, oh eh.)

||: E        B  |            :|| Play 3 times
||: F#5  B5 F#5 |   B5 F#5 :||
```

Bridge 2

F#5

Well, vi'lence is an energy. (Oh eh, oh eh.)

Well, from here to eternity. (Oh eh, oh eh.)

Well, violence is an energy. (Oh eh, oh eh.)

Well, silence is the enemy,

So gimme, gimme revolution!

Interlude

‖: B   E   B | E   B   A :‖

Chorus 3

B   E   B
‖: Do you know the en - emy?

           E   B
Do you know your en - emy?

A B   E   B   F#
Well, gotta know the en - emy. (Rah, eh!) :‖ *Play 3 times*

Verse 3

B   E   B   E   B
Overthrow the eff - igy, the vast major - ity,

A B   E   B   F#
Well, burning down the fore - man of con - trol. (Oh eh, oh eh.)

B   E   B   E   B
Silence is the en - emy, against your ur - gency,

A B   E   B   F#   B
So rally up the de - mons of your soul. (Oh eh, oh eh.)

Jesus of Suburbia

(Jesus of Suburbia/City of the Damned/I Don't Care/ Dearly Beloved/Tales of Another Broken Home)

Words by Billie Joe
Music by Green Day

Melody:

I'm the son of rage and love, _

Db Bbm Gb Ab Fm Ab/C A G Cm Eb

I. Jesus of Suburbia

Verse 1

Db
   I'm the son of rage and love,

Bbm
   The Jesus of Suburbia.

     Gb
From the Bible of "none of the above,"

    Ab   **Db**
On a steady diet of   soda pop and Ritalin.

Bbm   **Gb**
   No one ever died from my sins in hell

As far as I can tell,

     Ab
At least the ones I got away with.

Pre-Chorus 1

       Gb   **Ab**
But there's nothing wrong with me.

     Gb   **Ab**
This is how I'm s'posed to be

     Gb   **Ab**
In the land of make be - lieve

               Db Ab Gb Db Ab Gb
That don't believe in me.

Verse 2	**D♭** Get my television fix	

D♭
Get my television fix

B♭m
Sitting on my crucifix.

G♭
The living room in my private womb,

A♭
While the moms and Brads are away.

D♭
To fall in love and fall in debt

B♭m
To alcohol and cigarettes

G♭
And Mary Jane to keep me insane

A♭
And doing someone else's cocaine.

Pre-Chorus 2   *Repeat Pre-Chorus 1*

Outro 1

| **D♭** | | **B♭m** | | |
| **G♭** | | **A♭** | | |

Ooh.

| **D♭** | | **Fm** | | |
| **B♭m** | **A♭** | **G♭** | **A♭** | |

II. City of the Damned

Verse 3

      Db   **Ab/C**
At the center of the earth in the parking lot

      Bbm   **Ab**
Of the Seven Eleven where I was taught

Gb   **Ab**
  The motto was just a lie.

      Db
It says "Home is where your heart is."

   Ab/C
But what a shame 'cause

Bbm   **Ab**
Everyone's heart doesn't beat the same.

Gb   **Ab**
  We're beating out of time.

Chorus 3

Bbm   **Ab**
   City of the dead

Db   **Gb**
  At the end of an - other lost highway.

Bbm   **Ab**   **Gb**
  Signs mis - leading to no - where.

Bbm   **Ab**
  City of the damned,

Db   **Gb**
  Lost children with dirty faces today.

Bbm   **Ab**   **Gb**
  No one really seems to care.

Verse 4	**Db** **Ab/C** I read the graffiti in the bathroom stall

Db   **Ab/C**

Verse 4   I read the graffiti in the bathroom stall

       Bbm   **Ab**

Like the Holy Scriptures of the shopping mall.

Gb   **Ab**

   And so it seemed to con - fess.

    Db   **Ab/C**

It didn't say much but it only confirmed

       Bbm   **Ab**

That the center of the earth is the end of the world.

Gb   **Ab**

   And I could really care less.

Chorus 4   *Repeat Chorus 1*

III. I Don't Care

Interlude

Ab	**Db**	**Ab**	**Db**	
Gb	**Db**	**Ab**		‖

Chorus 5

    Ab   **Db**

‖: I don't care if you don't...

Ab   **Db**

I don't care if you don't...

Gb   **Db**   **Ab**

I don't care if you don't care. :‖ *Play 4 times*

Gb Ab   **Db**   **A Ab Db A Ab Db A Ab Db A Ab**

I   don't care.

Verse 5

Db   A Ab
Ev'ryone's so full of shit,

Db   A   Ab
Born and raised by hy - po - crites.

Db   A Ab
Hearts recycled but never saved

Db   A Ab
From the cradle to the grave.

Db   A   Ab
We are the kids of war and peace

Db   A Ab
From Anaheim to the Middle East.

Db   A Ab
We are the stories and disciples of

Db   A Ab
The Jesus of Suburb - ia.

Chorus 6

Gb   Ab Db Ab
Land of make be - lieve,

Gb   Ab   Db Ab
And it don't be - lieve in me.

Gb   Ab Db Ab
Land of make be - lieve,

Gb   Ab   Gb Ab
And I don't be - lieve and I   don't

 Db   Gb Ab
‖: Care. (Whoo! Whoo! Whoo!) I don't :‖ *Play 4 times*

|Db | Ab| | | | G‖
Care.

IV. Dearly Beloved

Verse 6

A♭
Dearly Beloved, are you listening? Cm

D♭   A♭   E♭
I can't remember a word that you were saying.

A♭   Cm
Are we demented or am I disturbed?

D♭   A♭   E♭
The space that's in between in - sane and inse - cure.

A♭   Cm D♭ A♭ E♭
(Ohh.   Ohh.   )

A♭   Cm
Oh, therapy, can you please fill the void?

D♭   A♭   E♭
Am I retarded or am I just over - joyed?

A♭   Cm
Nobody's perfect and I stand accused,

D♭   A♭   E♭
For lack of a better word and that's my best ex - cuse.

A♭   Cm D♭ A♭ E♭
(Ohh.   Ohh.   )

V. Tales of Another Broken Home

Intro   ‖:Ab   Gb Db|Ab   Gb Db:‖

              Ab
Verse 7   To live and not to breathe

              Is to die in tragedy.

              To run, to run away

              To find what you believe.
                   Db Ab Db Ab Db   Ab Eb   Ab Eb Ab Eb
              And I   leave be - hind
                   Db Ab Db Ab Db   Ab Eb Ab Eb Ab Eb
              This hur - ri - cane of fuck - ing lies.

              Ab
Verse 8   I lost my faith to this,

              This town that don't exist.

              So I run, I run away

              To the light of masochists.
                   Db Ab Db Ab Db   Ab Eb   Ab Eb Ab Eb
              And I   leave be - hind
                   Db Ab Db Ab Db   Ab Eb Ab Eb Ab Eb
              This hur - ri - cane of fuck - ing lies.
                   Db Ab Db Ab Db   Ab Eb   Ab Eb Ab Eb
              And I   walked this line
                  Db   Ab Db Ab Db   Ab Eb Ab Eb Ab Eb
              A mill - ion and one fuck - ing times.   But not this time.
              |Ab   Gb Db|Ab   Gb Db|

Guitar Solo ‖:A♭   G♭ D♭|A♭   G♭ D♭ |
| A♭   G♭ D♭|A♭   G♭ D♭:‖
‖: D♭ A♭ D♭ A♭ D♭ A♭ | E♭ A♭ E♭ A♭ E♭   :‖

Bridge

Fm   E♭   A♭   D♭
I don't feel any shame, I won't apolo - gize

　　　　　　　E♭   A♭
When there ain't nowhere you can go.

D♭   E♭   A♭   D♭
Running away from pain when you've been victim - ized

　　　　　　　E♭
Tales from an - other broken...

Outro 2

A♭   G♭   D♭ A♭   G♭   D♭
(Home) You're leav - ing,   you're leav - ing,

A♭   G♭   D♭ A♭   G♭   D♭
You're leav - ing,   are you leav - ing,

| A♭   G♭ D♭|A♭   G♭ D♭ |A♭   ‖
Home?

King for a Day

Words by Billie Joe
Music by Billie Joe and Green Day

Melody:

Start-ed at the age of four. _

E   C#m   A   B

Intro | E | C#m | E | C#m |

Verse 1

E   C#m
Started at the age of four.

E   C#m
My mother went to the grocery store.

E   C#m
Went sneaking through her bedroom door

E   C#m
To find something in a size four.

Pre-Chorus 1

A   B
Sugar and spice and ev'rything nice

   A   B
Wasn't meant for only girls.

A   B
G.I. Joe in pantyhose

  A   B
Is making room for the one and only

Chorus 1

E   C#m
King for a day, princess by dawn.

E   C#m
King for a day in a leather thong.

E   C#m
King for a day, princess by dawn.

A   B   E C#m E C#m
Just wait 'til all the guys get a load of me.

Verse 2

E   C#m
My daddy threw me in therapy.
E   C#m
He thinks I'm not a real man.
E   C#m
Who put the drag in the drag queen?
E   C#m
Don't knock it until you've tried it.

Pre-Chorus 2   *Repeat Pre-Chorus 1*

Chorus 2   *Repeat Chorus 1*

Interlude   ‖: E | C#m | E | C#m :‖ *Play 3 times*

Pre-Chorus 3   *Repeat Pre-Chorus 1*

Chorus 3

    E   C#m
‖: King for a day, princess by dawn.
E   C#m
King for a day in a leather thong. :‖ *Play 3 times*
E   C#m
King for a day, princess by dawn.
A   B
Just wait 'til all the guys,
A   B
Just wait 'til the guys,
A   B
Just wait 'til all the guys get a load of me.

Outro   ‖: E | C#m | E | C#m :‖ *Play 4 times*
| E |

Last of the American Girls

Words by Billie Joe
Music by Green Day

Melody:

She pats her make-up on

B   E   F#   B7   Em

Verse 1

          B   **E**
She puts her makeup on like graffiti on the walls of the heartland.

          B   **F#**
She's got her little book of conspiracies right in her hand.

          B   **E**
She is paranoid, endangered species headed into ex - tinction.

          B   **F#**   **B**
She is one-of-a-kind. Well, she's the last of the American girls.

Verse 2

          B   **E**
She wears her overcoat for the coming of the nuclear winter.

          B   **F#**
She is riding her bike like a fugitive of critical mass.

          B   **E**
She's on a hunger strike for the ones who won't make it for dinner.

          B   **F#**
She makes enough to survive for a holiday working-class.

Chorus 1

    B   B7   E   Em

She's a runaway of the es - tablishment incorpor - ated.

        B

She won't co - operate.

       F#   B   E B E B E B E

Well, she's the last of the American girls.

Verse 3

        B   E

She plays her vinyl records, singing songs on the eve of de - struction.

        B   F#

She's a sucker for all the criminals breaking the laws.

        B   E

She will come in first for the end of Western civili - zation.

        B   F#

She's an endless war, she's a hero for the lost cause.

Chorus 2

    B   B7   E   Em

Like a hurricane in the heart of devas - tation.

        B

She's a nat'ral disaster.

      F#   B   E B E B E B E

She's the last of the American girls.

Guitar Solo   ‖: B | | E | |

                | B | | F# | :‖

Chorus 3

        B   B7   E   Em

She puts her makeup on like graf - fiti on the walls of the heartland.

           B   B7   F#

She's got her little book of con - spiracies right in her hand.

        B   B7   E   Em

She will come in first for the end of Western civili - zation.

        B   F#   B   E

She's a nat'ral disaster. She's the last of the American girls.

B E   B E B E   B E

  Oh, yeah.   All right.

B E   B E B E B

  Oh, yeah.

GREEN DAY

Longview

Words by Billie Joe
Music by Green Day

Melody:

I sit a - round __ and watch

Tune down 1/2 step:
(low to high) E♭-A♭-D♭-G♭-B♭-E♭

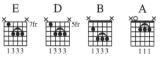

E   D   B   A

Intro   ‖: E | D | E | D   :‖

Verse 1
```
        E       D               E               D
        I sit a - round and watch the tube, but nothing's on.
        E           D               E           D
        I change the channels for an hour or two,
        E               D               E
        Twiddle my thumbs just for a bit.
                    D               E
        I'm sick of all the same old shit,
                D               E
        In a house with unlocked doors,
                        D
        And I'm fucking lazy.
```

                          B   A   E   B
Chorus 1   Bite my lip and close my eyes.

                                    A   E
                          Take me a - way to paradise.

                          B   A   E   B
                          I'm so damn bored I'm going blind

                                        A   E D E D
                          And I smell like shit.

                          E   D   E   D
Verse 2   Peel me off this Velcro seat and get me moving.

                          E   D   E   D
                          I sure as hell can't do it by myself.

                          E   D   E
                          I'm feeling like a dog in heat

                                       D   E
                          Barred in - doors from the summer street.

                                       D   E   D
                          I locked the door to my own cell and I lost the key.

                          B   A   E   B
Chorus 2   Bite my lip and close my eyes.

                                    A   E
                          Take me a - way to paradise.

                          B   A   E   B
                          I'm so damn bored I'm going blind

                                        A
                          And I smell like shit.

                          E   D
Bridge   I got no motivation.

                          E   D
                          Where is my motivation?

                          E   D
                          No time for a motivation.

                          E   D
                          Smoking my inspiration.

Interlude	|B	|A E	|B	|A E |
	|B	|A E	|B	|A |
	|E	|D	|E	|D |

Verse 3

```
E        D              E              D
   I sit a - round and watch the phone but no one's calling.

E          D          E          D
   Call me path - etic, call me what you will.

E            D          E              D            E
   My mother says to get a job, but she don't like the one she's got.

              D            E              D    A
   When mastur - bation's lost its fun you're fucking lonely.
```

Chorus 3

```
B          A      E      B
   Bite my lip and close my eyes.

              A      E
   Take me a - way to paradise.

B            A      E    B
   I'm so damn bored I'm going blind

              A      E
   And lonely - ness has to suffice.

B          A      E      B
   Bite my lip and close my eyes,

                A      E
   Oh, slipping a - way to paradise.

B          A      E      B
   Some say quit or I'll go blind,

                A
   But it's just a myth.
```

Outro   ‖: E   \|D   \|E   \|D   :‖ *Repeat and fade*

Macy's Day Parade

Words by Billie Joe
Music by Billie Joe and Green Day

Melody:

To-day's the Ma-cy's Day Pa-rade. _

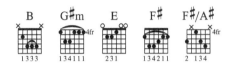

	B	G#m	E	F#	F#/A#
	1 3 3 3	1 3 4 1 1 1 (4fr)	2 3 1	1 3 4 2 1 1	2 1 3 4 (4fr)

Intro |B | | |

Verse 1

B
Today's the Macy's Day Parade.
  G#m
The night of the living dead is on its way,
E   F#   B
With the credit re - port for duty call.
                    G#m
It's a lifetime guarantee, stuffed in a coffin

"Ten percent more free."
E   F#   B
Red light special at the mauso - leum.

Pre-Chorus 1

E
Give me something that I need,
F#   E
Satisfaction guaranteed to you.

What's the consolation prize?
F#   B
Economy sized dreams of hope.

Verse 2

    B
When I was a kid I thought

 G#m
I wanted all the things that I haven't got.

E   F#   B
Oh, but I learned the hardest way.

            G#m
Then I realized what it took

                          E
To tell the diff'rence between thieves and crooks.

    F#   B
Let's learn, me and you.

Pre-Chorus 2

   E
Give me something that I need,

F#
Satisfaction guaranteed.

Chorus 1

          B   F#/A#   G#m
'Cause I'm thinking about a brand-new hope,

    F#   E
The one I've never known.

         F#   B
'Cause now I know it's all that I wanted.

Instrumental ‖: B | | G#m | |
                | E | F# | B | :‖

Pre-Chorus 3

E
What's the consolation prize?
F#   B
Economy sized dreams of hope.
E
Give me something that I need,
F#
Satisfaction guaranteed.

Chorus 2

              B   F#/A#   G#m
'Cause I'm thinking about a brand-new hope,
   F#   E   F#
The one I've never known and where it goes.
              B   F#/A# G#m
And I'm thinking 'bout the only   road,
   F#   E   F#
The one I've never known and where it goes.
              B   F#/A#   G#m
And I'm thinking 'bout a brand-new hope,
   F#   E   F#   B
The one I've never known 'cause now I know it's all that I wanted.

Minority

Words by Billie Joe
Music by Billie Joe and Green Day

Melody:

I want to be the mi - nor - i - ty.

C   G   Fmaj7   F   C*   F*   G*   Am   E   B

32 1   21 34   321   3211   1333   134211   134211   231   231   1333

Intro | C   G | Fmaj7 C | G | F   C |

Chorus 1

  C*   F*   G* F*
I want to be the mi - nori - ty.

  C*   F*   G* F*
I don't need your au - thori - ty.

  C*   F*   G* F*
Down with the moral ma - jori - ty.

      C*   F*   G* F*
'Cause I want to be the mi - nori - ty.

Verse 1

  C* G*   F*   C*
I pledge allegiance to the under - world.

          G*   F*   G*
One nation under - dog there of which I stand alone.

  C*   G*   F*   C*
A face in the crowd, un - sung against the mold.

        F*   G*   C*
Without a doubt, singled out, the only way I know.

Chorus 2

<pre>
        C*   F*   G*   F*
'Cause I want to be the mi - nori - ty.

C*   F*   G*   F*
I don't need your au - thori - ty.

C*   F*   G*   F*
Down with the moral ma - jori - ty.

        C*   F*   G*   F*
'Cause I want to be the mi - nori - ty.
</pre>

Bridge 1

<pre>
Am   E F* C*
   Stepped out of the line

Am   E   F*   G*
   Like a sheep runs from the herd.

Am   E F*   C*
   Marching out of time

Am   F* G*
   To my own beat now

                    B
The only way I know.
</pre>

Verse 2

<pre>
     C*   G* F*   C*
One light, one mind flashing in the dark.

              G*   F*   G*
Blinded by the silence of a thousand broken hearts.

      C*   G* F*   C*
"For crying out loud," she screamed unto me.

              F*   G*
A free-for-all, fuck 'em all. "You are your own sight."
</pre>

Chorus 3   *Repeat Chorus 2*

Bridge 2	|Am	E|F*	C*	|Am	E	|F*	G*	|

Bridge 2
\|Am   E\|F*   C* \|Am   E \|F* G* \|
\|Am   E\|F*   C* \|Am   F*\|G*   \|
\| B\|

Interlude
\|C* G* \|F*   C* \| G* \|F*   G* \|

Verse 3   *Repeat Verse 2*

Chorus 4

      C*   F*   G* F*
'Cause I want to be the mi - nori - ty.

C* F*   G* F*
I don't need your au - thori - ty.

C*   F*   G* F*
Down with the moral ma - jori - ty.

      C*   F*   G* F*
'Cause I want to be the mi - nori - ty.

   C*   F*   G* F*
‖: I want to be the mi - nori - ty. :‖ ***Play 4 times***

Outro   *Repeat Intro*

The Saints Are Coming

Words and Music by
Stuart Adamson and Richard Jobson

Melody:

There is a house in New Or - leans, _

Em   Em/D   Bm   Em*   F#7sus4   Bm/D   F#/C#   Bm*   G5   Em/G

Intro   ‖: Em   Em/D | Bm   :‖

Verse 1

      Em Em/D Bm
There is a house in New Orleans,

      Em   Em/D Bm
They call the Rising Sun.

      Em   Em/D Bm
It's been the ruin of many a poor boy,

      Em   Em/D   Bm
And God, I know I'm one.

    Em   Em/D
I cried to my Daddy on the telephone,

    Bm   Em   Em/D
How long now, until the clouds unroll and you come down?

    Bm
The line went.

      Em   Em/D   Bm
But the shadows still remain since your descent, your descent.

Interlude   ‖: Em* | F#7sus4 | Bm/D | F#/C# :‖

GREEN DAY

Verse 2

Em*   Bm/D
I cried to my daddy on the telephone,

Em* Bm/D Bm*
How long   now,

      Em*   Bm/D
'Til the clouds unroll and you come home?

Em* Bm/D Bm*
The line went.

      Em*   Bm/D
But the shadows still remain since your descent,

Em* Bm/D Bm*
Your de - scent.

Em   Em/D
Whoa! Cha! Hey!

Chorus 1

     Em*   G5   Em*   G5
The saints are coming, the saints are coming.

Em   Em/D
I say no matter how I try, I realize there's no reply.

Em*   G5   Em*   G5
The saints are coming, the saints are coming.

Em   Em/D   Em   N.C.
I say no matter how I try, I realize there's no re - ply.

Bridge

Em*	F#7sus4	Bm/D	F#/C#	
Ooh, _____			ooh.	

Em*	F#7sus4	Bm/D	F#/C#	
			Ooh.	

Em*	F#7sus4	Bm/D	F#/C#	
Ooh, _____			ooh.	

Em*	F#7sus4	Bm/D	F#/C#	

Verse 3

        Em*   **Bm/D**
A drowning sorrow floods the deepest grief,

Em* Bm/D Bm*
How long   now?

          Em*   **Bm/D**
Until the weather change con - demns belief,

Em* Bm/D Bm*
How long   now?

          Em*   **Bm/D**
When the night watchman lets in ___ the thief,

Em* Bm/D Bm*
What's wrong now?

Em   **Em/D**
Whoa! Cha! Hey!

Chorus 2

        Em*   **G5**   **Em***   **G5**
The saints are coming, the saints are coming.

  Em   **Em/D**
I say no matter how I try, I realize there's no reply.

    Em*   **G5**   **Em***   **G5**
The saints are coming, the saints are coming.

  Em   **Em/G**
I say no matter how I try, I realize there's no reply.

  Em   **Em/G**
I say no matter how I try, I realize there's no reply.

  Em   **Em/G**   **Em**
I say no matter how I try, I realize there's no re - ply.

Nice Guys Finish Last

Words by Billie Joe
Music by Billie Joe and Green Day

Melody:

Nice guys fin-ish last.

A E B E* F#

Intro

A		E	A B	A E
	A B	A E	A B	A E
	A E*	A E		

Verse 1

E
Nice guys finish last. You're running out of gas.
　　　B　　　　　　　　　　　E　　A
Your sympathy will get you left be - hind.

Sometimes you're at your best when you feel the worst.
　　　B　　　　　　　　　　　　　　　　E
You feel washed up, like piss going down the drain.

Pre-Chorus 1

A　　　　　　　　　　　　　E
Pressure cooker, pick my brain and tell me I'm insane.
A　　　　　　　　　E
I'm so fucking happy, I could cry.
A
Ev'ry joke can have its truth,
　　　E
But now the joke's on you.
　F#　　　　　　　　　　　B
I never knew you're such a funny guy.

Chorus 1

　　　E　　　　A
Oh, nice guys finish last,
　　　E　　　　　　A
When you are the out - cast.
　　　E　　　　　　A
Don't pat yourself on the back,
　　　　　　B　　A
You might break your spine.

Verse 2

E
Living on command. You're shaking lots of hands.

     B   E
You're kissing up and bleeding all your trust.

E
Taking what you need. Bite the hand that feeds.

     B   E
You'll lose your memory and you got no shame.

Pre-Chorus 2   *Repeat Pre-Chorus 1*

Chorus 2

     E   A
Oh, nice guys finish last,

       E   A
When you are the out - cast.

        E   A
Don't pat yourself on the back,

            B
You might break your spine.

          A
Oh, nice guys finish last,

       E   A
When you are the out - cast.

        E   A
Don't pat yourself on the back,

           B   A
You might break your spine.

Instrumental

```
| E   A B |    A E |   A B |    A E |
|     A B |    A E |     A |     F# |
|       B |        |       |        |
```

Chorus 3   *Repeat Chorus 2*

Outro

```
| E     |  A E |
```

Redundant

Words by Billie Joe
Music by Billie Joe and Green Day

Melody:

We're liv - ing in _____ rep - e - ti - tion.

A   A/G#   A/G   F#   Bm   D   E5   E   G5

Intro

|A |A/G# |A/G |F# |
|Bm |D |A | E5 |

Verse 1

```
       A         D      A    D A
    We're living in repe - tition.
                   D              E    G5
    Content in the same old shtick a - gain.
    A            D              A       D A
       Now routine's turning to con - tention.
                   D            E
    Like a produc - tion line going over and over and over, roller coaster.
```

Chorus 1

```
         A                A/G#
    Now I cannot speak. I've lost my voice.
    A/G            F#
    Speechless and re - dundant.
            Bm           D
    'Cause I love you's not e - nough.
            A     E5
    I'm lost for words.
```

Verse 2

```
    A         D              A       D A
    Choreo - graphed and lack of passion.
              D            E    G5
    Proto - types of what we were.
    A        D          A         D A
    One full circle 'till I'm nauseous.
                D              E
    Taken for granted now. I've waste, faked it, ate it. Now I hate it.
```

Chorus 2

```
            A                A/G♯
    'Cause I cannot speak. I've lost my voice.
    A/G              F♯
    Speechless and re - dundant.
            Bm             D
    'Cause I love you's not e - nough.
              A    E5
    I'm lost for words.
```

Instrumental

```
| A        | D      | A     D | A         |
| F♯       | Bm     | E       |     G5    |
| A        | D      | A       |           |
| F♯       | Bm     | E       |           |
```

Chorus 3

```
            A                A/G♯
||: Now I cannot speak. I've lost my voice.
    A/G              F♯
    Speechless and re - dundant.
            Bm             D
    'Cause I love you's not e - nough.
              A
    I'm lost for words. :||
```

Outro

```
| A        | A/G♯   | A/G     | F♯        |
```

She

Words by Billie Joe
Music by Green Day

She, ___   she screams in   si - lence.

Tune down 1/2 step:
(low to high) Eb-Ab-Db-Gb-Bb-Eb

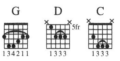

Intro   ‖: G | :‖

Verse 1

G   D
She, she screams in silence.

        C   G
A sullen riot penetrating through your mind.

        D   C
Waiting for a sign to smash the silence

                        G
With the brick of self-con - trol.

Chorus 1

D   C   G
Are you locked up in a world that's been planned out for you?

D   C   G
Are you feeling like a social tool without a use?

C   G   C   G
Scream at me until my ears bleed.

    C   G   D
I'm taking heed just for you.

Verse 2

```
        G           D          C
She, she's figured out all her doubts
                             G      C G
Were someone else's point of view.
                    D              C
Waking up this time to smash the silence
                          G      C G
With the brick of self-con - trol.
```

Chorus 2   *Repeat Chorus 1*

Interlude

```
‖: G        |        | D        |            |
   | C        |        | G    C G |        :‖
```

Chorus 3

```
D                              C                    G
Are you locked up in a world that's been planned out for you?
D                      C           G
Are you feeling like a social tool without a use?
C      G      C      G
Scream at me until my ears bleed.
      C      G          D      G
I'm taking heed just for you.
```

Stuck with Me

Words by Billie Joe
Music by Green Day

Melody:

I'm not part of your ___ e - lite, ___

Tune down 1/2 step:
(low to high) Eb-Ab-Db-Gb-Bb-Eb

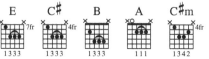

E   C#   B   A   C#m

Intro   ‖: E | C# B A | | :‖

Verse 1
   E   B
I'm not part of your elite, I'm just alright.

   A   B   A   B
Class structures waving colors, bleeding from my throat.

   E   B
Not subservient to you, I'm just alright.

   A   B   A   B
Down classed by the powers that be, give me loss of hope.

Chorus 1
   C#m   A E
Cast out, buried in a hole.

   C#m   A   E
Struck down, forcing me to fall.

   C#m   A   E
Destroyed, giving up the fight.

         A   B   E
Well, I know I'm not al - right.

Verse 2	**E** **B**

Verse 2

E   **B**
What's my price and will you pay it if it's al - right?

A   **B**   **A**   **B**
Take it from my dignity and waste it 'till it's dead.

E   **B**
Throw me back into the gutter 'cause it's alright.

A   **B**   **A**   **B**
Find another pleasure fucker, drag them down to hell.

Chorus 2   *Repeat Chorus 1*

Interlude   ‖: E | C♯ B A | | :‖ *Play 4 times*
                      | B | | | |

Chorus 3   *Repeat Chorus 1*

21st Century Breakdown

Words by Billie Joe
Music by Green Day

Born in - to Nix - on, I was raised in hell, _

Tune down 1/2 step:
(low to high) Eb-Ab-Db-Gb-Bb-Eb

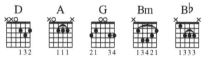

D   A   G   Bm   Bb

| **Intro** | ‖: D A   \| :‖ *Play 8 times* |
| | ‖: D   \| A G :‖ |

Verse 1

D   A   G
Born into Nixon, I was raised in hell,

D   A   G
A welfare child where the Teamsters dwelled.

D   A   G
The last one born and the first one to run,

D   A G
My town was blind from refin - ery sun.

Pre-Chorus 1

Bm   G
My generation is zero,

Bm   G   A
I never made it as a working class hero.

Chorus 1

D   A   G
Twenty-first century breakdown,

D   A   G
I once was lost but never was found.

D   A   G
I think I'm losing what's left of my mind

        D   A   G
To the twentieth century deadline.

D   A G D   A G
Ooh.

Verse 2

D   A   G
  I was made of poison and blood,

D   A   G
  Condemnation is what I understood.

D   A   G
  Video games to the tower's fall,

D   A   G
  Homeland security could kill us all.

Pre-Chorus 2

Repeat Pre-Chorus 1

Chorus 2

D   A   G
Twenty-first century breakdown,

D   A   G
I once was lost but never was found.

D   A   G
I think I'm losing what's left of my mind

        D   A   G
To the twentieth century deadline.

| Interlude 1 | ‖: A   \| \| \| :‖ *Play 4 times* |

Verse 3

A   D
We are the class of, the class of 'thirteen,

A   D
Born in the year of humility.

A   D
We are the desperate in the deadline,

A   D
Raised by the bastards of nineteen-sixty-nine.

| Interlude 2 | ‖: D   \| \| \| :‖ |

Verse 4

D   G   A D
My name is no one, the long lost son,

                  A
Born on the Fourth of Ju - ly.

D   G   A D
Raised in the era of heroes and cons,

                 A
Who left me for dead or a - live.

D   G   A D
I am a nation, a worker of pride.

              A
My debt to the status quo.

      D   G   A D
The scars on my hands and a means to an end

           A
Is all that I have to show.

| Interlude 3 | ‖: D   \| G \| D   \| G :‖ |

Verse 5

```
D                        G        A D
I swallowed my pride and I choked on my faith.
                         A
I've given my heart and my soul.
D                        G        A D
I've broken my fingers and lied through my teeth,
                         A
The pillar of damage con - trol.
D                              G       A     D
I've been to the edge and I've have thrown the bouquet
                              A
Of flowers left over the grave.
D                       G       A D
I sat in the waiting room, wasting my time
                         A
And waiting for Judgment Day.
```

Bridge

```
G       A D   G       A D
Praise lib - er - ty, the "freedom to o - bey"
    G         A     D
Is the song that stran - gles me.
    G           A G A G A G
Well, don't cross the line.
```

Interlude 4

```
|A       |         |         |         |
|D    A  |Bm  A  |G   B♭  |D        |
```

Outro

```
    D      A     Bm
Oh, dream, A - merica, dream.
    A      G      B♭        D
I can't even sleep from light's early dawn.
           A     Bm
Oh, scream, A - merica, scream.
    A          G       B♭      N.C.(D)
Be - lieve what you see from heroes and cons.
```

---

21 Guns

Words and Music by David Bowie,
John Phillips, Billie Joe
and Green Day

Melody:

Do you know __ what's worth fight - ing for __

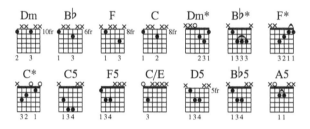

Intro   ‖:Dm B♭ |F C :‖

Verse 1

Dm*   B♭*   F*   C*
Do you know what's worth fighting for

Dm*   B♭*   F*   C*
When it's not worth dying for?

Dm*   B♭*   F*   C*
Does it take your breath away

B♭*   C*
And you feel ___ yourself suffocat - ing?

Dm*   B♭*   F*   C*
Does the pain weigh out the pride

Dm*   B♭*   F*   C*
And you look for a place to hide?

Dm*   B♭*   F*   C*
Did some - one break your heart inside?

B♭*   C5
You're in ru - ins.

F5 N.C. C/E   N.C.   D5
One,   twenty-one guns.

N.C. C5   Bb5
      Lay down your arms.

F5   C5
Give up the fight.

F5 N.C. C/E   N.C.   D5
One,   twenty-one guns.

N.C. C5   Bb5
      Throw up your arms

F5   C5   Bb5 F5 C5
Into the sky, ____ you and I.

Verse 2

Dm*   Bb* F*   C*
    When you're at the end of the road

Dm*   Bb*   F*   C*
   And you lost all sense of control.

Dm*   Bb*   F*   C*
   And your thoughts have taken their toll

                     Bb*   C*
When your mind ____ breaks the spirit of your soul.

Dm* Bb*   F*   C*
   Your faith walks on broken glass

Dm*   Bb*   F*   C*
   And the hangover doesn't pass.

Dm*   Bb* F*   C*
   Nothing's ever built to last.

              Bb*   C5
You're in ru - ins.

Chorus 2   *Repeat Chorus 1*

GREEN DAY   **73**

Bridge

D5   Bb5 F5   C5
Did you try to live on your own

D5   Bb5   F5   A5
When you burned down the house and home?

D5   Bb5   F5   A5
Did you stand too close to the fire

      Bb5   C5
Like a li - ar looking for forgive - ness from a stone?

Interlude 1

‖: F5 C/E |D5 C5 |Bb5 F5 |C5   :‖
|Bb5 F5 |A5 |

Interlude 2

Repeat Intro

Verse 3

Dm*   Bb*   F*   C*
When it's time to live and let die

Dm*   Bb*   F*   C*
And you can't get an - other try,

Dm*   Bb*   F*   C*
Something inside this heart has died.

       Bb*
You're in ru - ins.

Chorus 3

F5 N.C. C/E N.C.   D5
One,   twenty-one guns.

N.C. C5   Bb5
     Lay down your arms.

F5   C5
Give up the fight.

F5 N.C. C/E N.C.   D5
One,   twenty-one guns.

N.C. C5   Bb5
     Throw up your arms

F5   C5
Into the sky.

Chorus 4

Repeat Chorus 1

¡Viva la Gloria!

Words by Billie Joe
Music by Green Day

Melody:

Hey, Glo-ri - a, ___

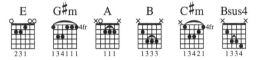

E G#m A B C#m Bsus4

Intro

```
        E          G#m       A              E
        Hey, Gloria, ___ are you standing close to the edge?
                    G#m       A              B
        Look out to the setting sun,     the brink of your vision.
        E      G#m    A          E
        Eternal youth is a landscape of a lie.
                    G#m            A              B
        The cracks of my skin can prove,     as the years will testify.
        C#m                    G#m
        Say your prayers and light a fire.
        A              E   B
        We're gonna start a war.
        C#m            G#m
        Your slogans a gun for hire.
        A          B
        It's what we've waited for.
        E          G#m       A              E
        Hey, Gloria, ___ this is why we're on the edge.
                    G#m            A          E
        The fight of our lives been drawn to     this undying love.
```

Chorus 1

<pre>
E   G#m
Gloria, viva la Gloria.

C#m   A
   You blast your name in graf - fiti on the walls.

Falling through broken glass
         E   B   C#m
That's slashing through your spirit

A   B
   I can hear it like a jilted crowd.
E   G#m
Gloria, where are you, Gloria?
C#m   A
   You found a home in all your scars and ammunition.
                          E   B   C#m
You made your bed in salad days among - st the ruins.
A   B
   Ashes to ashes of our youth.
</pre>

Verse

<pre>
E   G#m   C#m
   She smashed her knuckles into winter.

A   E   B
   As autumn's wind fades into black.
E   G#m   C#m
   She is the saint of all the sinners,

A   E   B
   The one that's fallen through the cracks.
             A   B
So don't put away your burning light.
</pre>

Chorus 2

E   G#m
Gloria, where are you, Gloria?

C#m   A
   Don't lose your faith to your lost naivete.

                                 E   B   C#m
Weather the storm and don't look back on last No - vember,

A   B
   When your banners were burning down.

E   G#m
Gloria, viva la Gloria.

C#m   A
   Send me your amnesty down to the broken hearted.

                         E   B C#m
Bring us the season that we always will remember.

A   B
Don't let the bonfires go out.

Outro

   A   E A   E
So, Gloria, ____   send out your message

   A   E   B   Bsus4 B
Of   the light that shadows in the night.

A   E A   E
Gloria, ____ where's your undying ____ love?

A   E   B   E
   Tell me the story of your life, your life.

Waiting

Words and Music by Billie Joe,
Green Day and Anthony Hatch

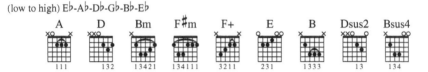

Tune down 1/2 step:
(low to high) Eb-Ab-Db-Gb-Bb-Eb

A	D	Bm	F#m	F+	E	B	Dsus2	Bsus4
111	132	13421	134111	3211	231	1333	13	134

Intro

      A   D
I've been waiting a long time

Bm   D
For this moment to come.

      A   D   Bm D
I'm destined for anything at all.

Verse 1

      A   D   Bm
Downtown lights will be shining on me

D   A   D   Bm D
Like a new diamond ring out under the midnight hour.

      A   D
Well, no one can touch me now.

Bm D
And I can't turn my back,

      A   D   Bm D
It's too late, ready or not at all.

Chorus 1

<pre>
      F#m   F+
Well, I'm so much closer

      E   B
Than I have ever known.

          D A D N.C.
Wake up.
</pre>

Verse 2

<pre>
A   D   Bm
Dawning of a new era calling,

D   A
Don't let it catch you falling,

D   Bm   D
Ready or not at all.

      A   D
Well, so close, enough to taste it.

Bm   D   A
Almost I can embrace this feeling

D   Bm   D
On the tip of my tongue.
</pre>

Chorus 2

<pre>
      F#m   F+
Well, I'm so much closer

      E   B
Than I have ever known.
</pre>

<pre>
Wake up.
|D   A   D | A D A D A |
|D   A   D | A D A D A |
                    Better   thank your
|D   A   D | A D A D A |
 Luck - y   stars.
|D   A   D A |E |
 Sure, hey, hey.
</pre>

| *Guitar Solo* | \|A | \|D | \|Bm | \|D | \| |
| | \|A | \|D | \|B | \|D | \| |

Chorus 3   *Repeat Chorus 2*

Interlude   \|A   \|Dsus2   \|Bsus4   \|Dsus2   \|

A   Dsus2
I've been ____ waiting a lifetime

Bsus4   Dsus2
  For this ____ moment to come.

    A   Dsus2   **Bsus4 Dsus2**
I'm destined ____ for anything at all.

A   D

Verse 3   Dumbstruck, colour me stupid.

Bm   D
Good luck, you're gonna need it

A   D   Bm   D
Where I'm going if I get there at all.

    A   D Bm D

Outro   Wake up.

    A   D Bm D
Better thank your lucky stars.

Warning

Words by Billie Joe
Music by Billie Joe
and Green Day

Melody:

This is a pub - lic ser - vice an - nounce-ment.

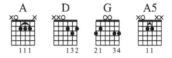

A	D	G	A5
1 1 1	1 3 2	2 1 3 4	1 1

Intro

‖: A   D | G   D :‖   *Play 4 times*

Verse 1

        A   D
This is a public ser - vice announcement.

G   D   A D G D
This is on - ly a test.

   A   D   G   D   A D G D
E - mergen - cy, e - vacuation, protest.

         A   D   G   D
May im - pair your a - bility to operate ma - chinery.

A   D G   D
Can't quite tell just what it means to me.

A   D   G   D
Keep out of reach of children, don't you talk to strangers.

      A   D G   D
Get your philoso - phy from a bumper sticker.

Chorus 1

```
A     D  G       D     A D G D
Warn - ing: Live without warning.

          A     D  G        D
Let's see a warn - ing: Live without warning.

A  D  G       D
      Without.   Alright.
```

Interlude 1

```
|A5           |            |            |            |
|A     D  |G     D  |A     D  |G     D  |
```

Verse 2

```
A     D      G           D       A D G D
Better homes and safety sealed com - munities?

A        D        G       D     A D G D
Did you re - member to pay the u - tilities?

A     D          G       D
Caution: Police line. You better not cross.

          A         D  G          D
Is it the cop or am I the one that's really dangerous?

A         D        G           D
Sanitation, expiration date, question ev'rything?

A     D          G       D
Or shut up and be the victim of au - thority.
```

Chorus 2

```
A     D  G       D     A D G D
Warn - ing: Live without warning.

          A     D  G        D      A D G D
Let's see a warn - ing: Live without warning.

          A     D  G        D      A D G D
Let's see a warn - ing: Live without warning.

          A     D  G        D
Let's see a warn - ing: Live without warning.

A  D  G       D
      Without.   Alright.
```

| *Interlude 2* | ‖: A5 | :‖ |

Verse 3

A5
Better homes and safety sealed communities?

Did you remember to pay the utilities?

A   D   G   D
Caution: Police line. You better not cross.

        A   D G   D
Is it the cop or am I the one that's really dangerous?

A   D   G   D
Sanitation, expiration date, question ev'rything?

A   D   G   D
Or shut up and be the victim of au - thority.

Chorus 3

A   D G   D   A D G D
Warn - ing: Live without warning.

        A   D G   D   A D G D
Let's see a warn - ing: Live without warning.

        A   D G   D   A D G D
Let's see a warn - ing: Live without warning.

        A   D G   D   A D G D
Let's see a warn - ing: Live without warning.

Outro

      A   D
This is a public service announcement.

G   D   A
This is only a test.

Wake Me Up When September Ends

Words by Billie Joe
Music by Green Day

Melody:

Sum - mer _ has come and passed, _

Chord diagrams: G5, G5/F#, G5/E, G5/D, C, Cm, Em, Bm, D, G5*, D/F#, Dsus4

Intro

‖: G5 | :‖

Verse 1

G5   G5/F#
Summer has come and passed,

  G5/E   G5/D
The innocent can never last.

C   Cm   G5
Wake me up when September ends.

          G5/F#
Like my father's come to pass,

G5/E   G5/F#
Seven years has gone so fast.

C   Cm   G5
Wake me up when September ends.

Chorus 1

Em   Bm   C   G5 G5/F#
Here comes the rain again, falling from the stars.

Em   Bm   C   D
Drenched in my pain again, be - coming who we are.

Verse 2

G5   G5/F#   G5/E   G5/D
As my mem - ory rests, but never forgets what I lost.

C   Cm   G5
Wake me up when September ends.

Interlude 1

‖: G5 | :‖ *Play 3 times*

Verse 3

G5   G5/F♯
Summer has come and passed,
    G5/E   G5/D
The innocent can never last.
C   Cm   G5*
Wake me up when September ends.
G5   G5/F♯
Ring out the bells again,
G5/E   G5/D
Like we did when spring began.
C   Cm   G5* D/F♯
Wake me up when September ends.

Chorus 2

Em   Bm   C   G5* D/F♯
Here comes the rain again, falling from the stars.
Em   Bm   C   D
Drenched in my pain again, be - coming who we are.

Verse 4

G5   G5/F♯   G5/E   G5/D
As my mem - ory rests, but never forgets what I lost.
C   Cm   G5* D/F♯
Wake me up when September ends.

Guitar Solo

Em	Bm	C	G5* D/F♯
Em	Bm	C	Dsus4
D	Dsus4	D	

Interlude 2

‖: G5 | :‖

Verse 5

G5   G5/F♯
Summer has come and passed,
    G5/E   G5/D
The innocent can never last.
C   Cm   G5*
Wake me up when September ends.
G5   G5/F♯
Like my father's come to pass,
G5/E   G5/F♯
Twenty years has gone so fast.

Outro

   C   Cm   G5*
‖: Wake me up when September ends. :‖ *Play 3 times*

GREEN DAY   **85**

Walking Contradiction

Words by Billie Joe
Music by Green Day

Melody:

Do as I say, not ___ as I

Tune down 1/2 step:
(low to high) E♭-A♭-D♭-G♭-B♭-E♭

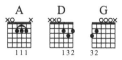

Intro   ‖: A | :‖

Verse 1
    A   D   G   A
Do as I say, not as I do
                         D   G   A
Because the shit's so deep you can't run away.
              D   G   A
I beg to differ, on the contrary,
               D   G   A
I agree with ev'ry word that you say.
          D   G   A
Talk is cheap and lies are expensive,
             D   G   A
My wallet's fat and so is my head.
          D   G   A
Hit and run, and then, I'll hit you again,
             D G   A
A smart ass but, I'm playing dumb.

Interlude 1   ‖: A D G | A   :‖

Verse 2

```
A         D    G    A
Standards set and broken all the time,
          D    G    A
Control the chaos behind the gun.
          D  G
Call it as I see it,
A         D    G          A
Even if I was born deaf, blind, and dumb.
          D    G    A
Losers winning big on the lottery,
          D    G    A
Rehab rejects still sniffing glue.
          D    G    A
Constant refu - tation with myself,
          D  G   A
I'm a victim of a catch twenty-two.
```

Chorus 1

```
D  G  A
        I have no belief,
D  G  A
        But I believe
      D    G    A
I'm a walking contra - diction.
      D    G    A
And I ain't got no right.
```

Interlude 2   *Repeat Interlude 1*

Verse 3   *Repeat Verse 1*

Chorus 2

```
  D  G  A
‖:      I have no belief,
D  G  A
        But I believe
      D    G    A
I'm a walking contra - diction.
      D    G    A
And I ain't got no right.  :‖
```

Outro   ‖: A   D G │ A   :‖ *Play 4 times*

Welcome to Paradise

Words by Billie Joe
Music by Green Day

Melody:

Dear moth-er, can __ you hear __ me

Tune down 1/2 step:
(low to high) Eb-Ab-Db-Gb-Bb-Eb

E   D   A   G   B   C   G*   F#   F

1333 1333 111 134211 1333 1333 1333 1333 1333

Intro

‖: E |D   A   :‖   *Play 4 times*

Verse 1

E   D   E
　Dear mother, can you hear me whining?
　　　　　　　D   G   B
It's been three whole weeks since that I have left your home.
E   D   E
　The sudden fear has left me trembling
　　　　　　　D   G   B
'Cause now it seems that I am out here on my own
　　　　　　G   B
And I'm feel - ing so a - lone.

Chorus 1

E   G   A   C
Pay attention to the cracked streets and the broken homes.
E   G   B
　Some call it slums, some call it nice.
E   G   A   C
I want to take you through a wasteland I'd like to call my own.
E B   E   D A E D A
　Welcome to paradise.

Verse 2

```
E              D              E
A gunshot rings out at the station,
        D           G          B
Another urchin snaps and left dead on his own.
E              D              E
It makes you wonder why I'm still here.
              D           G          B
For some strange reason, it's now feeling like my home,
        G       B
And I'm never gonna go.
```

Chorus 2

```
E           G              A           C
Pay attention to the cracked streets and the broken homes.
E           G           B
Some call it slums, some call it nice.
    E           G                 A           C
I want to take you through a wasteland I'd like to call my own.
E  B         E         D  A  E  D  A  E  D  A  E  D  A
   Welcome to paradise.
```

Interlude 1   ‖: E   G* | F♯   F   :‖   *Play 20 times*

Verse 3

```
E              D              E
Dear mother, can you hear me laughing?
        D                 G          B
It's been six whole months since that I have left your home.
E              D              E
It makes me wonder why I'm still here.
              D           G          B
For some strange reason, it's now feeling like my home,
        G       B
And I'm never gonna go.
```

Chorus 3

```
E           G              A           C
Pay attention to the cracked streets and the broken homes.
E           G           B
Some call it slums, some call it nice.
    E           G                 A           C
I want to take you through a wasteland I'd like to call my own.
E  B         E         D  A  E  D  A
   Welcome to paradise.
    E         D  A  E  D  A  E
Oh, paradise.
```

When I Come Around

Words by Billie Joe
Music by Green Day

Melody:

I heard you cry - in' loud —

Tune down 1/2 step:
(low to high) E♭-A♭-D♭-G♭-B♭-E♭

G   D   Em   C   A5   C5

Intro   ‖: G   D | Em   C   :‖   *Play 3 times*

Verse 1

```
G   D               Em    C
  I heard you cryin' loud
G       D           Em    C
  All the way across town.
              G                 D
You've been searching for that someone,
          Em                C
And it's me, out on the prowl.
    G       D           Em      C
As you sit a - round feeling sorry for yourself,
G       D               Em   C
  Well, don't get lonely now
G       D                       Em  C
  And dry your whining eyes.
              G               D                Em
I'm just roaming for the moment sleazing my backyard,
        C           G
So don't get so uptight,
              D           Em      C
You been thinking about ditching me.
```

Chorus 1

```
A5                    C5
   No time to search the world around

A5                            C5
   'Cause you know where I'll be found

                        G  D  Em  C  G  D  Em  C
When I come around.
```

Verse 2

```
G  D            Em    C
   I heard it all be - fore,

G     D                   Em   C
   So don't knock down my door.

     G        D       Em            C
I'm a loser and a user so I don't need no ac - cuser

     G           D            Em        C
To try and slag me down, because I know you're right.

G     D          Em   C
   So go do what you like.

G      D         Em    C
   Make sure you do it wise.

        G                D
You may find out that your self-doubt

        Em            C
Means nothing was ever there.

        G            D            Em    C
You can't go forcing something if it's just not right.
```

Chorus 2   *Repeat Chorus 1*

Interlude   ‖: G   D |Em C :‖

Chorus 3

```
A5                    C5
   No time to search the world around

A5                            C5
   'Cause you know where I'll be found


When I come around.

   G  D  Em  C
‖:                     When I come around.  :‖  Play 3 times
```

Outro |G   D |Em C |

When It's Time

Words and Music by
Billie Joe

Melody:

Words get trapped in my mind, —

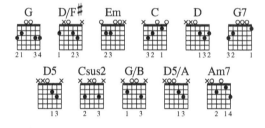

Verse 1

G   D/F#
Words get trapped in my mind,

              Em   C
Sorry I don't take ____ the time to feel the way I do.

              G   D
'Cause the first ____ day you came into my life,

                          G   D
My time ticks around ____ you.

G   D/F#
But then I need your voice

              Em   C
As the key to un - lock all the love that's trapped in me.

              G   D   G   G7
So tell me when it's time ____ to say I love ____ you.

Chorus 1

    C   G

    All I want is you to understand,

      D   G

That when I take your hand, it's 'cause I want to.

C   G

We are all born in a world of doubt.

                   D

But there's no doubt,

              D5 Csus2 G/B D5/A

I figured out ____ I   love you.

Intro   ‖: G   D Em | | C   G D | :‖

Chorus 2   *Repeat Chorus 1*

Verse 2

G   D/F♯

   I feel lonely for ____ all the losers

     Em   C

That ____ will never take the time to say

          G

What's real - ly on their mind,

     D/F♯   G   D

Instead, ____ they just hide a - way.

G   D/F♯

   Yet, they'll never have ____ someone like you

     Em   C

To ____ guide them and help them along the way,

              G   D   G

Or tell them when it's time ____ to say I love ____ you.

               D

So tell me when it's time

          C   G/B Am7 G

To say I love ____ you.

Guitar Chord Songbooks

Each book includes complete lyrics, chord symbols, and guitar chord diagrams.

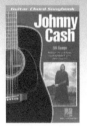   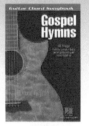 

Acoustic Hits
More than 60 songs: Against the Wind • Name • One • Southern Cross • Take Me Home, Country Roads • Teardrops on My Guitar • Who'll Stop the Rain • Ziggy Stardust • and more.
00701787 ....$14.99

Acoustic Rock
80 acoustic favorites: Blackbird • Blowin' in the Wind • Layla • Maggie May • Me and Julio down by the Schoolyard • Pink Houses • and more.
00699540...............................$21.99

Alabama
50 of Alabama's best: Angels Among Us • The Closer You Get • If You're Gonna Play in Texas (You Gotta Have a Fiddle in the Band) • Mountain Music • When We Make Love • and more.
00699914...............................$14.95

The Beach Boys
59 favorites: California Girls • Don't Worry Baby • Fun, Fun, Fun • Good Vibrations • Help Me Rhonda • Wouldn't It Be Nice • dozens more!
00699566...............................$19.99

The Beatles
100 more Beatles hits: Lady Madonna • Let It Be • Ob-La-Di, Ob-La-Da • Paperback Writer • Revolution • Twist and Shout • When I'm Sixty-Four • and more.
00699562...............................$17.99

Bluegrass
Over 40 classics: Blue Moon of Kentucky • Foggy Mountain Top • High on a Mountain Top • Keep on the Sunny Side • Wabash Cannonball • The Wreck of the Old '97 • and more.
00702585...............................$14.99

Johnny Cash
58 Cash classics: A Boy Named Sue • Cry, Cry, Cry • Daddy Sang Bass • Folsom Prison Blues • I Walk the Line • Ring of Fire • Solitary Man • and more.
00699648...............................$17.99

Children's Songs
70 songs for kids: Alphabet Song • Bingo • The Candy Man • Eensy Weensy Spider • Puff the Magic Dragon • Twinkle, Twinkle Little Star • and more.
00699539...............................$16.99

Christmas Carols
80 Christmas carols: Angels We Have Heard on High • The Holly and the Ivy • I Saw Three Ships • Joy to the World • O Holy Night • and more.
00699536...............................$12.99

Christmas Songs
80 songs: All I Want for Christmas Is My Two Front Teeth • Baby, It's Cold Outside • Jingle Bell Rock • Mistletoe and Holly • Sleigh Ride • and more.
00119911...............................$14.99

Eric Clapton
75 of Slowhand's finest: I Shot the Sheriff • Knockin' on Heaven's Door • Layla • Strange Brew • Tears in Heaven • Wonderful Tonight • and more.
00699567 ....$19.99

Classic Rock
80 rock essentials: Beast of Burden • Cat Scratch Fever • Hot Blooded • Money • Rhiannon • Sweet Emotion • Walk on the Wild Side • and more.
00699598 ....$18.99

Coffeehouse Hits
57 singer-songwriter hits: Don't Know Why • Hallelujah • Meet Virginia • Steal My Kisses • Torn • Wonderwall • You Learn • and more.
00703318 ....$14.99

Country
80 country standards: Boot Scootin' Boogie • Crazy • Hey, Good Lookin' • Sixteen Tons • Through the Years • Your Cheatin' Heart • and more.
00699534 ....$17.99

Country Favorites
Over 60 songs: Achy Breaky Heart (Don't Tell My Heart) • Brand New Man • Gone Country • The Long Black Veil • Make the World Go Away • and more.
00700609 ....$14.99

Country Hits
40 classics: As Good As I Once Was • Before He Cheats • Cruise • Follow Your Arrow • God Gave Me You • The House That Built Me • Just a Kiss • Making Memories of Us • Need You Now • Your Man • and more.
00140859 ....$14.99

Country Standards
60 songs: By the Time I Get to Phoenix • El Paso • The Gambler • I Fall to Pieces • Jolene • King of the Road • Put Your Hand in the Hand • A Rainy Night in Georgia • and more.
00700608 ....$12.95

Cowboy Songs
Over 60 tunes: Back in the Saddle Again • Happy Trails • Home on the Range • Streets of Laredo • The Yellow Rose of Texas • and more.
00699636 ....$19.99

Creedence Clearwater Revival
34 CCR classics: Bad Moon Rising • Born on the Bayou • Down on the Corner • Fortunate Son • Up Around the Bend • and more.
00701786 ....$16.99

Jim Croce
37 tunes: Bad, Bad Leroy Brown • I Got a Name • I'll Have to Say I Love You in a Song • Operator (That's Not the Way It Feels) • Photographs and Memories • Time in a Bottle • You Don't Mess Around with Jim • and many more.
00148087 ....$14.99

Complete contents listings available online at www.halleonard.com

Crosby, Stills & Nash
37 hits: Chicago • Dark Star • Deja Vu • Marrakesh Express • Our House • Southern Cross • Suite: Judy Blue Eyes • Teach Your Children • and more.
00701609.................................$16.99

John Denver
50 favorites: Annie's Song • Leaving on a Jet Plane • Rocky Mountain High • Take Me Home, Country Roads • Thank God I'm a Country Boy • and more.
02501697 ....$17.99

Neil Diamond
50 songs: America • Cherry, Cherry • Cracklin' Rosie • Forever in Blue Jeans • I Am...I Said • Love on the Rocks • Song Sung Blue • Sweet Caroline • and dozens more!
00700606 ....$19.99

Disney
56 super Disney songs: Be Our Guest • Friend like Me • Hakuna Matata • It's a Small World • Under the Sea • A Whole New World • Zip-A-Dee-Doo-Dah • and more.
00701071 ....$17.99

The Doors
60 classics from the Doors: Break on Through to the Other Side • Hello, I Love You (Won't You Tell Me Your Name?) • Light My Fire • Love Her Madly • Riders on the Storm • Touch Me • and more.
00699888 ....$17.99

Eagles
40 familiar songs: Already Gone • Best of My Love • Desperado • Hotel California • Life in the Fast Lane • Peaceful Easy Feeling • Witchy Woman • more.
00122917 ....$16.99

Early Rock
80 classics: All I Have to Do Is Dream • Big Girls Don't Cry • Fever • Itsy Bitsy Teenie Weenie Yellow Polkadot Bikini • Let's Twist Again • Lollipop • and more.
00699916 ....$14.99

Folk Pop Rock
80 songs: American Pie • Dust in the Wind • Me and Bobby McGee • Somebody to Love • Time in a Bottle • and more.
00699651 ....$17.99

Folksongs
80 folk favorites: Aura Lee • Camptown Races • Danny Boy • Man of Constant Sorrow • Nobody Knows the Trouble I've Seen • and more.
00699541 ....$14.99

40 Easy Strumming Songs
Features 40 songs: Cat's in the Cradle • Daughter • Hey, Soul Sister • Homeward Bound • Take It Easy • Wild Horses • and more.
00115972 ....$16.99

Four Chord Songs
40 hit songs: Blowin' in the Wind • I Saw Her Standing There • Should I Stay or Should I Go • Stand by Me • Turn the Page • Wonderful Tonight • and more.
00701611 ....$14.99

Glee
50+ hits: Bad Romance • Beautiful • Dancing with Myself • Don't Stop Believin' • Imagine • Rehab • Teenage Dream • True Colors • and dozens more.
00702501 ....$14.99

Gospel Hymns
80 hymns: Amazing Grace • Give Me That Old Time Religion • I Love to Tell the Story • Shall We Gather at the River? • Wondrous Love • and more.
00700463 ....$14.99

Grand Ole Opry®
80 great songs: Abilene • Act Naturally • Country Boy • Crazy • Friends in Low Places • He Stopped Loving Her Today • Wings of a Dove • dozens more!
00699885 ....$16.95

Grateful Dead
30 favorites: Casey Jones • Friend of the Devil • High Time • Ramble on Rose • Ripple • Rosemary • Sugar Magnolia • Truckin' • Uncle John's Band • more.
00139461 ....$14.99

Green Day
34 faves: American Idiot • Basket Case • Boulevard of Broken Dreams • Good Riddance (Time of Your Life) • 21 Guns • Wake Me Up When September Ends • When I Come Around • and more.
00103074 ....$14.99

Irish Songs
45 Irish favorites: Danny Boy • Girl I Left Behind Me • Harrigan • I'll Tell Me Ma • The Irish Rover • My Wild Irish Rose • When Irish Eyes Are Smiling • and more!
00701044 ....$14.99

Michael Jackson
27 songs: Bad • Beat It • Billie Jean • Black or White (Rap Version) • Don't Stop 'Til You Get Enough • The Girl Is Mine • Man in the Mirror • Rock with You • Smooth Criminal • Thriller • more.
00137847 ....$14.99

Billy Joel
60 Billy Joel favorites: • It's Still Rock and Roll to Me • The Longest Time • Piano Man • She's Always a Woman • Uptown Girl • We Didn't Start the Fire • You May Be Right • and more.
00699632 ....$19.99

Elton John
60 songs: Bennie and the Jets • Candle in the Wind • Crocodile Rock • Goodbye Yellow Brick Road • Sad Songs Say So Much • Tiny Dancer • Your Song • more.
00699732 ....$15.99

Ray LaMontagne
20 songs: Empty • Gossip in the Grain • Hold You in My Arms • I Still Care for You • Jolene • Trouble • You Are the Best Thing • and more.
00130337................................$12.99

Latin Songs
60 favorites: Bésame Mucho (Kiss Me Much) • The Girl from Ipanema (Garôta De Ipanema) • The Look of Love • So Nice (Summer Samba) • and more.
00700973 ....$14.99

Love Songs
65 romantic ditties: Baby, I'm-A Want You • Fields of Gold • Here, There and Everywhere • Let's Stay Together • Never My Love • The Way We Were • more!
00701043................................$14.99

Bob Marley
36 songs: Buffalo Soldier • Get up Stand Up • I Shot the Sheriff • Is This Love • No Woman No Cry • One Love • Redemption Song • and more.
00701704................................$17.99

Bruno Mars
15 hits: Count on Me • Grenade • If I Knew • Just the Way You Are • The Lazy Song • Locked Out of Heaven • Marry You • Treasure • When I Was Your Man • and more.
00125332 ....$12.99

Paul McCartney
60 from Sir Paul: Band on the Run • Jet • Let 'Em In • Maybe I'm Amazed • No More Lonely Nights • Say Say Say • Take It Away • With a Little Luck • and more!
00385035 ....$16.95

Steve Miller
33 hits: Dance Dance Dance • Jet Airliner • The Joker • Jungle Love • Rock'n Me • Serenade from the Stars • Swingtown • Take the Money and Run • and more.
00701146................................$12.99

Modern Worship
80 modern worship favorites: All Because of Jesus • Amazed • Everlasting God • Happy Day • I Am Free • Jesus Messiah • and more.
00701801 ....$16.99

Motown
60 Motown masterpieces: ABC • Baby I Need Your Lovin' • I'll Be There • Stop! In the Name of Love • You Can't Hurry Love • and more.
00699734 ....$17.99

Willie Nelson
44 favorites: Always on My Mind • Beer for My Horses • Blue Skies • Georgia on My Mind • Help Me Make It Through the Night • On the Road Again • Whiskey River • and many more.
00148273 ....$17.99

Nirvana
40 songs: About a Girl • Come as You Are • Heart Shaped Box • The Man Who Sold the World • Smells like Teen Spirit • You Know You're Right • and more.
00699762 ....$16.99

Roy Orbison
38 songs: Blue Bayou • Oh, Pretty Woman • Only the Lonely (Know the Way I Feel) • Working for the Man • You Got It • and more.
00699752 ....$17.99

Peter, Paul & Mary
43 favorites: If I Had a Hammer (The Hammer Song) • Leaving on a Jet Plane • Puff the Magic Dragon • This Land Is Your Land • and more.
00103013...................................$19.99

Tom Petty
American Girl • Breakdown • Don't Do Me like That • Free Fallin' • Here Comes My Girl • Into the Great Wide Open • Mary Jane's Last Dance • Refugee • Runnin' Down a Dream • The Waiting • and more.
00699883 ....$15.99

Pink Floyd
30 songs: Another Brick in the Wall, Part 2 • Brain Damage • Breathe • Comfortably Numb • Hey You • Money • Mother • Run like Hell • Us and Them • Wish You Were Here • Young Lust • and many more.
00139116 ....$14.99

Pop/Rock
80 chart hits: Against All Odds • Come Sail Away • Every Breath You Take • Hurts So Good • Kokomo • More Than Words • Smooth • Summer of '69 • and more.
00699538 ....$16.99

Praise and Worship
80 favorites: Agnus Dei • He Is Exalted • I Could Sing of Your Love Forever • Lord, I Lift Your Name on High • More Precious Than Silver • Open the Eyes of My Heart • Shine, Jesus, Shine • and more.
00699634 ....$14.99

Elvis Presley
60 hits: All Shook Up • Blue Suede Shoes • Can't Help Falling in Love • Heartbreak Hotel • Hound Dog • Jailhouse Rock • Suspicious Minds • Viva Las Vegas • and more.
00699633 ....$17.99

Queen
40 hits: Bohemian Rhapsody • Crazy Little Thing Called Love • Fat Bottomed Girls • Killer Queen • Tie Your Mother Down • Under Pressure • You're My Best Friend • and more!
00702395 ....$14.99

Red Hot Chili Peppers
50 hits: Californication • Give It Away • Higher Ground • Love Rollercoaster • Scar Tissue • Suck My Kiss • Under the Bridge • and more.
00699710 ....$19.99

The Rolling Stones
35 hits: Angie • Beast of Burden • Fool to Cry • Happy • It's Only Rock 'N' Roll (But I Like It) • Miss You • Not Fade Away • Respectable • Rocks Off • Start Me Up • Time Is on My Side • Tumbling Dice • Waiting on a Friend • and more.
00137716 ....$17.99

Bob Seger
41 favorites: Against the Wind • Hollywood Nights • Katmandu • Like a Rock • Night Moves • Old Time Rock & Roll • You'll Accomp'ny Me • and more!
00701147...................................$12.99

Carly Simon
Nearly 40 classic hits, including: Anticipation • Haven't Got Time for the Pain • Jesse • Let the River Run • Nobody Does It Better • You're So Vain • and more.
00121011...................................$14.99

Sting
50 favorites from Sting and the Police: Don't Stand So Close to Me • Every Breath You Take • Fields of Gold • King of Pain • Message in a Bottle • Roxanne • and more.
00699921 ....$17.99

Taylor Swift
40 tunes: Back to December • Bad Blood • Blank Space • Fearless • Fifteen • I Knew You Were Trouble • Look What You Made Me Do • Love Story • Mean • Shake It Off • Speak Now • Wildest Dreams • and many more.
00263755...............................$16.99

Three Chord Acoustic Songs
30 acoustic songs: All Apologies • Blowin' in the Wind • Hold My Hand • Just the Way You Are • Ring of Fire • Shelter from the Storm • This Land Is Your Land • and more.
00123860 ....$14.99

Three Chord Songs
65 includes: All Right Now • La Bamba • Lay Down Sally • Mony, Mony • Rock Around the Clock • Rock This Town • Werewolves of London • You Are My Sunshine • and more.
00699720 ....$17.99

Two-Chord Songs
Nearly 60 songs: ABC • Brick House • Eleanor Rigby • Fever • Paperback Writer • Ramblin' Man Tulsa Time • When Love Comes to Town • and more.
00119236...............................$16.99

U2
40 U2 songs: Beautiful Day • Mysterious Ways • New Year's Day • One • Sunday Bloody Sunday • Walk On • Where the Streets Have No Name • With or Without You • and more.
00137744...............................$14.99

Hank Williams
68 classics: Cold, Cold Heart • Hey, Good Lookin' • Honky Tonk Blues • I'm a Long Gone Daddy • Jambalaya (On the Bayou) • Your Cheatin' Heart • and more.
00700607 ....$16.99

Stevie Wonder
40 of Stevie's best: For Once in My Life • Higher Ground • Isn't She Lovely • My Cherie Amour • Sir Duke • Superstition • Uptight (Everything's Alright) • Yester-Me, Yester-You, Yesterday • and more!
00120862 ....$14.99

HAL•LEONARD®

Prices, contents and availability subject to change without notice.